A-10 Warthog

in action

by
Lou Drendel

squadron/signal publications

cover

A-10A of the 81st TFW with full anti-armor mission load of Maverick Missiles, Rockeyes, and ECM pod.

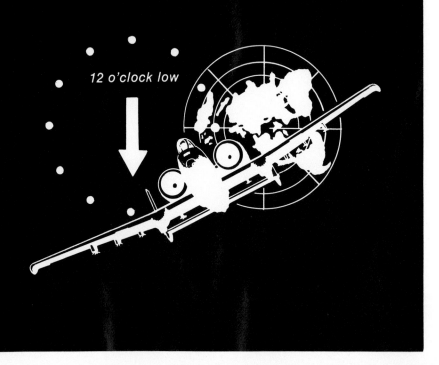

12 o'clock low

ISBN 0-89747-122-9

If you have any photographs of the aircraft, armor, soldiers or ships of any nation, particularly wartime snapshots, why not share them with us and help make Squadron/Signal's books all the more interesting and complete in the future. Any photograph sent to us will be copied and the original returned. The donor will be fully credited for any photos used. Please send them to: Squadron/Signal Publications, Inc., 1115 Crowley Dr., Carrollton, TX 75011-5010.

PHOTO CREDITS

USAF
Norman E. Taylor
Shinichi Ohtaki
Fairchild/Republic
Brian Rogers
Jerry Geer
Jim Sullivan
Ted Carlson
Charles B. Mayer
Duane Kasulka
Carlton Eddy
R.J. Archer
P. Bennett

It might almost be considered Machiavellian, for by all outward appearances, the **A-10 Thunderbolt II** is ugly, ungainly, the very antithesis of the modern warplane. But its looks are deceptive, for it is one of the deadliest, most efficient aerial killers ever to take to the sky.

The A-10's crews have continued the tradition of ignoring the official name of Republic products that goes back to World War II, when the **P-47 Thunderbolt** became the **Jug**. (Some would have you believe that Jug was short for **Juggernaut**, but few ever called the P-47 anything but just plain Jug...and it looked more like a Jug than a Juggernaut anyway.) Later, the **F-84 Thunderjet** became the **Hog**, and the F-105 drew a chorus of substitutes for the official "Thunderchief", **Ultra Hog**, **Lead Sled**, **Thunderthud** and just plain **Thud**. The A-10 Thunderbolt II has been re-christened **Warthog**, and there seems little doubt that that is the name it will carry ever more. (It looks more like a **Warthog** than a **Thunderbolt Two** anyway.)

But regardless of what they were called, those Republic built airplanes with the funny names had a way of becoming heroic when put to the test of combat. The **Jug** became the scourge of German fighters and supply columns during World War II, and the **Thud** carried 75% of the Air War to the North Vietnamese during **Rolling Thunder**. If the United States' policy of deterrance through preparedness keeps the peace, then the **Warthog** will not have to live up to its heritage in combat, but it will have accomplished a significant amount of the deterring because of its capability as the most effective aerial tank killer of all time.

A curious thing about the Warthog is its image among Air Force pilots. You would think that an airplane as unattractive as the A-10, which was designed to fly low and slow, would not encourage much enthusiasm among pilots. Quite the contrary has happened. When I first met Captain Al Whitley, in the fall of 1979, he was the high time A-10 pilot, having participated in much of the testing of the Thunderbolt II. He was emphatic about two things. First of all, he insisted that we refer to the airplane as the **"Warthog...not** the **Thunderbolt II"**. Secondly, he was convinced that the A-10 would become the most sought after pilot assignment in the Air Force. Al made the point that the very fact that the A-10 was mission-profiled to fly at low levels made it more fun to fly than almost any other airplane in the inventory. The mission is also one of the toughest and most dangerous, in war or peace. In war, the A-10 pilot will be right down in the weeds, mixing it up with every kind of air defense the enemy can throw at him. He will have to navigate to his target at low, low level, using terrain masking to avoid radar detection wherever possible, and he will have to do this by looking outside the airplane, map reading, and dead-reckoning (pending installation of a much sought-after inertial navigation set). If getting there is half the fun, then A-10 pilots are having plenty of fun in peacetime, as they hone their low level navigation skills. It is a challenging assignment, exactly the kind of job the typical fighter pilot revels in, and more and more of them are asking for **Warthog** assignment. And the A-10's less than sleek lines aren't likely to bother them, after all, **Nobody's sweetheart is ugly!**

Wood mock-up model constructed in the Fairchild Republic model shop during conceptual studies for the AX competition. (Fairchild Republic)

The prototype A-10 under construction at Republic's Long Island plant. Fairchild Republic was a sub-contractor to McDonnell Douglas on the F-4 Phantom, accounting for the numerous Phantom Phins in the background. (Fairchild Republic)

The idea for a pure close air support aircraft was first set forth in 1966 by Air Force Chief of Staff General John P. McConnell. After a tour of the war zone in Southeast Asia, he stated the need for an aircraft that would embody the best characteristics of the venerable A-1 Skyraider, and the yet-to-fly A-7D Corsair II, and would be cheaper to produce than either of them. In addition to the recognized **best characteristics of the A-1 and A-7**, the Air Force also wanted an airplane that would have STOL capability, from rough fields. They had few preconceived notions concerning configurations and powerplants, and in March 1967, Request For Proposals (RFP) went out to 21 companies for design studies. In May A-X study contracts were awarded to General Dynamics, Grumman Aircraft, Northrop and McDonnell Douglas, for preliminary design studies of the A-X specialized close air support aircraft.

Activity and funding were sluggish throughout much of the late sixties on the A-X, and it was not until May of 1970 that RFP's were issued to 12 companies for competitive prototype development. By the following August, six of the twelve had submitted proposals. They were: Boeing, Cessna, Fairchild, General Dynamics, Lockheed and Northrop. In December Fairchild and Northrop were selected to participate in competitive prototype evaluations. They each built two prototypes of their A-X designs, the first examples of which made their first flights in May, 1972. The Air Force designated the Northrop entry **A-9** and the Fairchild entry **A-10**.

Air Force testing of the A-9 and A-10 began at Edwards AFB in October, 1972. Pilots from Air Force Systems Command and Tactical Air Command flew the A-9 307.6 hours, the A-10 328.1 hours before the evaluations were completed in early December. In January 1973, the Air Force announced that the A-10 was the winner, having demonstrated itself to be almost twice as effective as a tank killer, while being 25% cheaper to operate.

On March 1, 1973 Fairchild Industries was awarded a $159,279,888 cost-plus-incentive-fee contract to continue prototype aircraft testing and to develop and build 10 pre-production aircraft. Concurrently, General Electric was awarded a $27,666,900 fixed-price-incentive-firm contract for development of 32 TF34 engines to power the A-10. The TF34 is the same engine that powers the Navy's S-3 Viking Anti-submarine Warfare Aircraft, so the technology was well in hand for the A-10's powerplant. Cost of the A-10 was expected to be $1.5 million per airplane, based on a buy of 600 copies, to be delivered at the rate of 20 per month, once production got underway. Costs were stated in 1970 dollars.

While development of the airframe was going on, two manufacturers were competing for the GAU-8 gun contract. Philco-Ford and General Electric had both submitted prototypes of a 30MM tank-killing gun to the Air Force's Armament Development and Test Center at Eglin AFB, Florida for testing. On June 21, 1973 the Air Force announced the completion of contract negotiations with General Electric, after having announced four days earlier that GE was the winner of the competition. They were awarded a $23,754,567 fixed-price-incentive-firm contract for three preproduction models to be used for quality testing and eight preproduction models to be installed in the A-10.

During its development and testing phase, the A-10 was subjected to a great deal of unfavorable scrutiny (as were most defense projects during this time period) by unfriendly congressional critics, whose desire to climb on the anti-war bandwagon outweighed any inclination to responsible planning for future defense. They suggested an additional fly-off competition, to be held between the A-4, A-7 and A-10. Since the performance characteristics of these airplanes was sufficiently dissimilar to effectively render almost impossible any objective structuring of such a fly-off under identical mission profiles, it was thought that such a fly-off would not be possible. There was a comparitive flight evaluation on the relative operational effectiveness of the **YA-10** and the A-7D, performing in the close support role, at Fort Riley, Kansas. Every professional must have known that the YA-10 would win this competition hands down, but the charade was carried out as a sop to the A-X critics.

On July 31, 1974 DOD released $39 million to proceed with initial production of 52 A-10s, subject to the provision that contrct options to procure a smaller quantity be kept open. Exactly three months later, the official military qualification tests were completed on the TF34-100 engines, and they were accepted for use in production aircraft. The following month the Air Force announced selection of the 333rd Tactical Fighter Training

Squadron, Davis-Monthan AFB, Arizona, as the first unit to receive the **A-10A**. Deliveries were to begin in April, 1976. On December 20th the Air Force was authorized to proceed with production of the 52 aircraft, through Fiscal Year 1975 and 1976.

Out in the high desert, at Edwards AFB, California, the testing of the A-10 was continuing, and in February, 1975 two milestones were marked. The prototypes passed a thousand hours of testing since their first flight and the first preproduction A-10 made its maiden flight. The first two prototypes would complete a total of 1,139.4 hours before being retired in April, and June, respectively.

The first production A-10 (Serial Number 75-00258) made its first flight at Republic's Farmingdale, N.Y. plant on October 21, 1975. On November 13, one of the preproduction airplanes successfully demonstrated the GAU-8/A 30MM cannon's effectiveness against a series of tank targets, including the Soviet T-62 main battle tank, at Nellis AFB, Nevada ranges.

As the Bi-Centennial year dawned, the A-10 was wowing 'em at Nellis and had already picked up the name that would stick, official naming contests to the contrary. They were calling it **Warthog** in honor of its general ugliness, and specifically because of the wart-like rivets that made its skin resemble that of *Phacohoerus aetheopicus*. In February DOD authorized the Air Force to get the production line cranked up to 15 aircraft per month, and the fourth production aircraft was delivered directly to the 355th TFTW at Davis-Monthan. In March the Air Force announced that the first operational Air Combat Wing to get the A-10 would be the 354th at Myrtle Beach AFB, S.C. That same month AFSC completed their testing of the A-10, turning it over officially to TAC.

The Warthog began its final operational test and evaluation at the 355th TFTW in August. It flew to England for the Farnborough Air Show in September, and afterward continued on to the Continent for a tour of key military installations, where USAFE was able to confirm that the A-10 was fully compatible with Third Generation Aircraft Protective Shelters. It was tested in the European battle scenario, working with OV-10 FAC's, during **Operation Reforger** in Germany before completing a 94 hour, 15,000 mile deployment.

Further testing of the A-10's ability to work in low ceiling/poor visibility conditions was conducted at Fort Lewis, Washington in November and December. Arctic testing was conducted the following month at Eielson AFB, Alaska, during **Operation Jack Frost**. In February two Warthogs demonstrated their surge capability, each flying 17 missions in an eleven hour period. Each mission covered 120 nautical miles, and consisted of dropping four 500 pound bombs, and making two 30MM strafe passes.

In April and May, 1977 four A-10s from the 333rd TFTS participated in **Red Flag 77-76/Irwin II**, staged on the Fort Irwin, California range. It was the largest exercise the A-10 had participated in up to that time, and provided the best insights yet on the A-10's operational effectiveness and ability to survive under the battle field conditions it was expected to encounter in a real shooting war. The A-10s operated from Bicycle Dry Lake, and coordinated their operations with Air Force, Navy, Marine Corps, and Army aircraft. Threats were simulated by the Nellis AFB range complex, which has the capability of simulating all known Warsaw Pact anti-aircraft threats, and by the Aggressor Squadron at Nellis. The A-10s were tracked with video tape machines through the optical view finders of the ZSU-23 and ZSU-57 AA sites. In 112 missions, the "enemy" was able to shoot down one A-10 with 23MM fire, one with an SA-6, and three fell to the Aggressor Squadron F-5s, which employed Soviet Tactics in their operations. No unusual maintenance problems were encountered, and average turn-around time for the A-10s was 15 to 20 minutes bet-

Another view of number one during construction. Note the vertical fin shape, which was changed on production models of the A-10. (Fairchild Republic)

(Right Middle and Right) The prototype was rolled out in the spring of 1972, and after the appropriate ceremonies, it was disassembled and transported to Edwards AFB, California, reassembled, and flown on its maiden flight by Sam Nelson, 10 May 1972. In the interest of safety, testing was done at Edwards AFB, though that caused a postponement of two weeks in the tightly scheduled flight test program, while the prototypes were disassembled and flown to Edwards in two C-124s. (Fairchild Republic)

The prototype on the ramp at Edwards during weapons testing. A minimum of composite alloys and Honeycomb structures were used in initial design of the A-10 in order to hold down costs and speed production. (Duane Kasulka via Jim Sullivan)

ween missions. Conditions on the dry lakebed were often harsh, with blowing sand forcing ground crew to don goggles and masks in order to work on the airplanes. The A-10 tactics consisted of a flight of two aircraft coordinating their attacks, one A-10 standing off and trying to bag the anti-aircraft defenses with its Maverick Missiles, while the second A-10 pressed in to within 4,000 feet to destroy tanks with its GAU-8 cannon. Results of the tests were enthusiastically received by the Air Force, as they more than proved the A-10's ability to survive and deliver in a tough combat scenario.

The first A-10 crash occurred at the Paris Air Show on 3 June. Fairchild Director of Flight Operations Howard W. (Sam) Nelson was completing the second of two loops when the aircraft developed a high sink rate. Nelson was unable to recover, and the aircraft struck the ground, bounced, hit again and disintegrated, killing its pilot. The accident was a tragic highlight of a development program that in all other ways was successful.

During June and July three A-10s from Davis-Monthan toured PACAF, demonstrating the burgeoning tactical prowess of the Warthog, and on 1 July the first operational squadron was activated at Myrtle Beach. The 356th TFS was combat ready a record three months later.

At about the same time, the 66th Fighter Weapons Squadron was reconstituted at Nellis AFB. The 66th's mission was to develop the A-10 Fighter Weapons Instructor Course, train A-10 pilots in advanced fighter tactics and weapons delivery, and develop and validate new tactics for the A-10. The 66th had formerly flown the F-105G **Wild Weasel**.

The first Operational Readiness Inspection of an A-10 unit took place in January 1978, when the 356th TFS deployed to the Savannah Air National Guard Field Training Site at Travis Field. Conditions were not the best, with cold gusty winds doing their best to

hamper operations. In the four day ORI, the 24 Warthogs of the 356th flew 319 sorties, fired over 25,000 rounds of 30мм ammunition, and dropped 420 Mk 82 training bombs on the Fort Stewart Ranges. Maintenance personnel were able to keep the aircraft ready to fly when needed, and everyone was generally very impressed with the reliability and accuracy of the airplane.

In April, the A-10 Warthog was officially named **Thunderbolt II**, an event that was destined to live in obscurity, as everyone who had a working relationship with the airplane continued to call it **Warthog**.

As operational testing of the airplane continued, it became more and more obvious that it would not be possible to operate in the environment most likely to generate a future war—Europe—without an Inertial Navigation Set and an accurate radar altimeter. Smoke and ground haze, combined with low ceilings and rain, often reduce visibility to a mile or less in Central Europe. Trying to navigate to targets at 100 feet or less, at speeds in the neighborhood of 300 knots, called for sharp map reading, and careful avoidance of telephone poles! It was now obvious that the A-10 was all that the Air Force had wanted in a reliable Close Air Support (CAS) machine, and the next major step was training its pilots to perform the low level mission, without inducing high levels of fatigue, which might lead to fatal mistakes on that 7th or 8th sortie of the day. The logical answer was an Inertial Navigation Set (INS) and Radar Altimeter. This was going to add lots of bucks to the program, and the hue and cry went up immediately. "The Air Force had suckered Congress and the people into going along with what they insisted would be a cheap program, and now they were adding things to it that should have been there in the first place." The criticism was unfair, and unwarranted. The Air Force did want a simple system, and adding additional navigation equipment was not going to complicate it unnecessarily.

In August 1978, the 333rd TFTS began training A-10 pilots for the 81st TFW, which was due to accept its first European-based A-10s in January 1979. Under the program name **Ready Thunder**, the 92nd TFS **Avengers** began transition from the F-4D to the A-10. The same month, the 354th TFW became the first fully combat-ready A-10 wing in the Air

Force. The 354th was based at Myrtle Beach AFB, S.C., and their conversion from the A-7D to the A-10 had taken 13 months.

That fall was a busy time for the Warthog. A detachment of ten aircraft from Myrtle Beach participated in **Red Flag 79-1** at Fort Irwin, California, while another eight were travelling to Hawaii for **Cope Elite**, and still others were participating in **Joint Air Attack Team III** at Fort Knox and **Gallant Eagle** at Tyndall AFB, Florida. Throughout 1978, A-10s of the 354th TFW, 355th TFW and 57th FWW had travelled to Army Posts throughout CONUS, demonstrating the A-10's close support prowess for the troops it would be working with. At the end of the year, the new camouflage scheme of two shades of green and dark grey, called *Lizard*, was adopted after a series of tests had indicated that it was the best choice under likely operational conditions.

The first European based A-10 Squadron accepted its aircraft in January 1979 at RAF Bentwaters-Woodbridge, UK. The Squadron redeployed some of the airplanes immediately to a Forward Operating Location (FOL) at Sembach AB, Germany, so that they could participate in the US Army Field Training Exercise **Certain Sentinel**. They were joined by six airplanes from the 354th TFW, ferried across from Myrtle Beach. The Warthog's debut was an immediate success, as it demonstrated its ability to operate in some of the harshest European weather in years.

While the A-10 was entering operational combat units, the tactics it would employ were being developed by the 57th Fighter Weapons Wing. The 57th is based at Nellis AFB, but did a lot of travelling in order to coordinate its tactics with US Army Aviation units. Much of the book of A-10 tactics was developed in the Joint Attack Weapons System (JAWS) Tactics Development Evaluation. As the first aircraft designed specifically to work with "troops in contact", the A-10 would have to interact with Army scout and attack helicopters. The tactics developed consisted of basic coordination of these weapons. The basic rule of thumb developed gave the A-10s airspace from the treetops up, and the helicopters the space from the ground to the treetops. Both would use terrain masking as defensive tactics. The scout helicopter was expected to FAC for the A-10s, with the attack

The second prototype *YA-10A* as it appeared in November 1974, during spin testing. It is painted in overall gunship grey FS 36118. White wing and tail surface on left side only were for photographic definition during the tests. (USAF via Dave Mason)

helicopters staying *down* while the A-10s were attacking, then up as the A-10s pulled off the target, drawing enemy AAA, which could then be identified and attacked by the helicopters. This kind of coordination would assure maximum continuous pressure on the enemy, while simplifying command and control of defensive forces. The first of these exercises was so successful that a manual was generated, and continuation of the series was assured by both services.

In September 1979, the first A-10s were delivered to the Air National Guard. The 175th Tactical Fighter Group, of the Maryland Air National Guard was the first of the Air Guard to get the Warthog. Other Air Guard units to get the A-10 included the 174th TFW, Syracuse, N.Y., the 103rd TFG, Windsor Locks, CT., and the 104th TFG, Westfield, Mass.

Transition of the 81st TFW from the F-4D to the A-10 was completed in September 1979. The 81st was composed of the 92nd, 510th, 78th and 91st Tactical Fighter Squadrons. In the meantime, anti-armor tactics continued to develop under TASVAL at Fort Hunter Liget, California. The DOD announced that an attack of 70 tanks, using the tree-studded hills for cover had resulted in the "destruction" of 60 of them. TASVAL A-10s and TOW-armed helicopter gunships, equipped with lasers and sensors, which were linked to a central computer, scored hits based upon known parameters of the weapons utilized.

In a show of force, staged to demonstrate the Carter Administration's displeasure with the "unacceptable" Russian combat brigade in Cuba, Exercise **Coronet Loop** took place at Guantanamo Bay, Cuba in November, 1979. A-10s of the 353rd TFS deployed from Myrtle Beach AFB for the exercise, during which they practiced close support integration with the Marine Corps and air combat tactics offshore. Presumably, the folks at NAS Guantanamo were impressed. Also presumably, the Russians were not, since they are still in Cuba.

Early in 1980, the Air Force announced that the Air Force Reserve would begin operating the A-10. Scheduled to convert to the A-10 at that time were the 45th TFS at Grissom AFB, Indiana (from A-37s), and the 47th TFS at Barksdale AFB, Louisiana (also from A-37s). The 23rd TFW, England AFB, Louisiana was also scheduled to convert to A-10s (from A-7s).

As this is written, the Warthog continues to improve and refine its operational tactics through an on-going program of participation in exercises, worldwide, with the armed forces of the United States and its allies. Hopefully, we will not see the A-10 "In Action" in any scenario other than these, but if it is forced to fire its 30MM *Avenger* in anger, the Warthog will prove to be a formidable foe to those masses of enemy armor that worry military tacticians so mightily.

30MM
GAU-8A

(Top) Special adjuncts to the spin test airplane included a spin-recovery drag chute and (right) special instrumentation to provide information on angle of attack, yaw, side slip angle, and pressure altimeter. (USAF via Dave Mason)

ESCAPAC
Ejection Seat

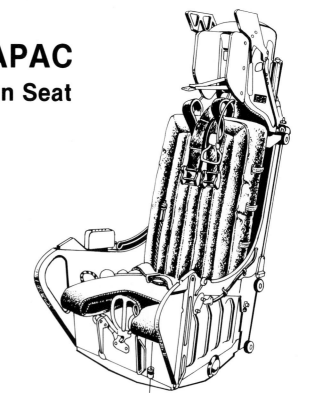

(Above left) Instrument panel. (Left bottom) Left console, and (below) right console make up the Hog Driver's office. Note that radios are mounted on the left console, while much of the right console is devoted to the environmental controls. (Fairchild Republic)

10

ACES II
Ejection Seat

Two ejection seats have been employed in the A-10 to date. The Escapac 1E-9 was installed initially. The seat assembly consists of six major components, including: the basic structural assembly forming the bucket, backrest and headrest; a survival kit, which the pilot sits on; the parachute, which provides the backrest; a ballistic haul-back inertial reel; a gyro controlled vernier-rocket for pitch stabilization; and, a man/seat separation rocket. From initiation of the ejection sequence until you are swinging under nylon takes 3.5 seconds if ejection takes place under 14,000 feet. You will leave the airplane within 0.3 seconds of pulling the handle! The ACES II seat is built by McDonnell Douglas and is capable of providing safe ejection at speeds and altitudes ranging from zero-zero up to 600 knots, and even inverted, down to within 155 feet of the ground! Both seats employ special stabilization rockets that minimize flailing of the pilot's limbs during high-speed or high G ejections. The parachute remains in the airplane and is connected to the pilot's torso harness by the risers, which also act as inertial reel shoulder harness. A lap belt completes the restraint system. In the event that the canopy might fail to jettison in the ejection sequence, canopy breakers on top of the headrest make through-the-canopy ejection possible. Cockpit access is via a self-contained boarding ladder.

Design Philosphy...

Why it looks that way.

The A-10 owes its very distinctive appearance to Fairchild's approach to engineering the Air Force's design requirements. The pod-mounted TF-34-100 engines were mounted away from each other and the fuselage to enhance survivability. If one engine is hit and chews itself up, or explodes, the chances are that it will not put the other engine out of action. Having the engines mounted high reduces their vulnerability to foreign object damage, caused by sticks and stones being sucked in on the ground. It also lessens the volume of dust kicked up by operations on unimproved fields. Mounting the engines away from the fuselage meant that the fuselage structure could be kept simple, strong, and uninterrupted, and it kept the engines away from volatile fuel bladders. Mounting the engines on the fuselage meant more hardpoints in the wings to hang ordnance on, and that those hardpoints could be rearmed while the engines were running, which cut turnaround time.

That big, tank-killing 30mm GAU-8 cannon is mounted on the centerline of the fuselage for good reason. The average recoil from one round is 10,000 pounds, and the gun will fire at rates of 2 to 4 thousand rounds per minute! Would that slew you sideways? You bet! Mounting the seven foot long cannon on the centerline forced Fairchild to offset the nose gear to the right, giving the Warthog a very distinctive head-on look while on the ground.

The wingtips are drooped to provide better lift at low speeds, and eliminate tip losses. The twin tails provide better low speed directional control, as well as serving to mask the IR signature of the engines. The podded wheel wells, reminiscent of the C-47 Gooney Bird with the main wheels hanging halfway out in the breeze, simplified landing gear design, and besides, drag is no big problem for the A-10.

If the A-10 lacks a lot of the compound curves that make modern airplanes look so sleek, it also lacks a big disadvantage of those types of airplanes. 98% of A-10 parts are interchangeable from airplane to airplane. (Contrasted with that, the F-4 has individually fitted canopies, wingtips, and stress panels.) Because the skin panels on the A-10 are not stressed, they can be repaired or replaced with virtually anything in the field to keep the airplane flying and fighting. The interchangeability of landing gears, ailerons, rudders, elevators, control actuators, and engines mean a lot of straight lines and uninspiring looks, but they also mean operational effectiveness.

Tail Development

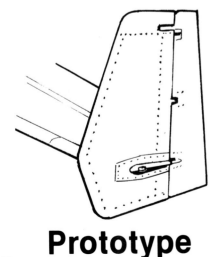

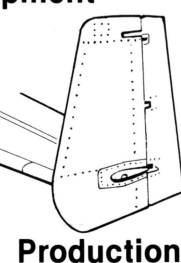

Prototype

Production

The first production A-10A (73-1664) as it appeared in mid-1975 during testing at Edwards. It is carrying a full complement of external fuel tanks. Overall gunship grey, with yellow and red test boom mounted in refueling receptacle. (Fairchild Republic)

Underside of wing with flaps extended. (Ted Carlson)

External Fuel Tanks

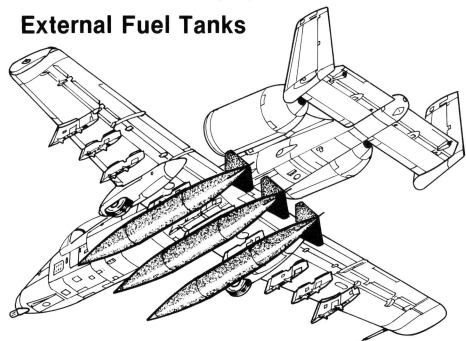

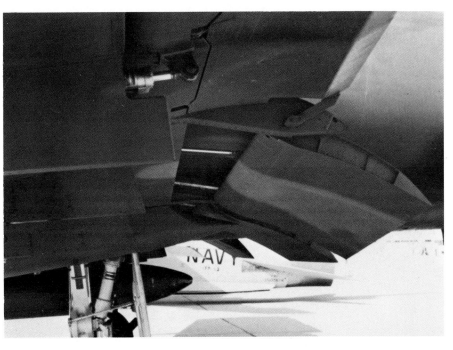

Design Philosophy...

Survivability

Studies done on combat losses in Vietnam and the 1967 Arab-Israeli War showed that 62% of losses occurred as a result of fuel fires and explosions, 18% were due to pilot incapacitation, and the balance were due to structural failure. The A-10's fuel tanks are lined with fire suppresant foam, which has protected the contents of the tanks from explosion through tests in which up to 300 rounds of high explosive incendiary ammunition was fired into the tanks. There are six fuel tanks in the A-10. The two wing tanks are the least protected, and mission profiles call for them to be emptied enroute to the target area. The other tanks are completely independent of each other and can be isolated. In the event that all six are holed, there are two large sumps at the bottom of the fuselage that will hold enough fuel for a 200 nautical mile flight.

The pilot is protected by a titanium-armor "bathtub" which is capable of repulsing direct hits from **23MM** and **57MM** shells. The bathtub makes up 47% of the total of 2,900 pounds of armor protection for the A-10's systems. An additional 37% is allocated for protection of the fuel system.

How much will it take to achieve a structural failure in the A-10? The wings and horizontal tail surfaces are protected by triple redundancy. There are three spars in each! The entire package is stressed for 7.3 G's positive, clean, or 5.0 G's fully loaded. It is capable of sustaining a 3.25 G turn at 275 knots, and with those big straight wings, it should be able to turn inside any enemy fighter without dumping its load first. And it will be able to stay within sight of the target while avoiding direct overflight of the target, where air defenses will be toughest. The GAU-8 cannon's trajectory is almost laser-flat, making it deadly at a range of 4,000 feet, capable of knocking out a tank at 6,000 with a well-placed shot, or able to destroy lightly armored vehicles at two miles!

Comparitive studies have shown that the A-10, while being twice as large, and a lot slower than the A-7, is actually only half as vulnerable to taking mortal damage. The Air Force is fond of advertising that the A-10 could lose **one engine**, **half the tail**, **two-thirds of a wing**, **and chunks of the fuselage...and still get home!**

Titanium Armor Plate "Tub"

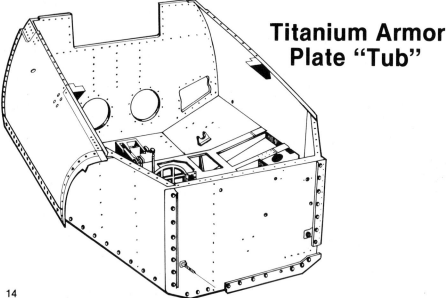

A-10 FUEL SYSTEM

▨	**Rigid, Reinforced Fire-Retardant Foam**
▨	**Reticulated, Flexible Interior Foam (25 PPI)**
☐	**Fuel Wets Skin (Non-Dangerous)**
▨	**Mil-P-46111 Non-Reticulated Flexible Foam**

Self-Seal Fuel Line Cover

Self-Sealer Level

Self-Seal Barrier

FWD

(Left) The first production A-10A as it was delivered to the 355th TFW in 1976 with serial number displayed as 50258.

(Below) It was later repainted to reflect more accurately the "76-0258" serial. It was finished in overall light ghost grey FS36375, with black codes and insignia. TAC badge is in standard colors. APU exhaust (under port engine only) has darkened the engine pod. (Fairchild Republic and Carlton Eddy via Jim Sullivan)

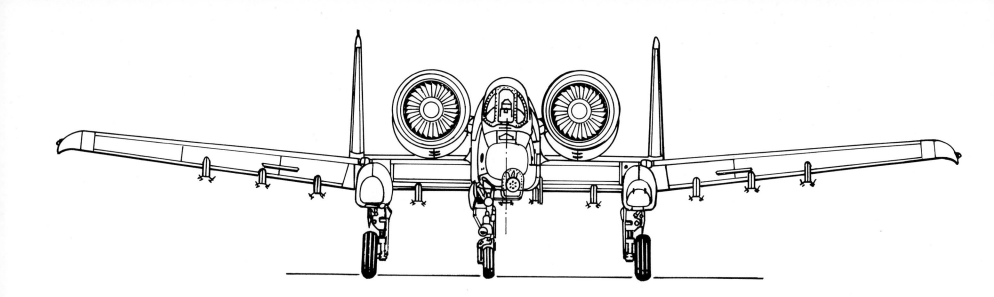

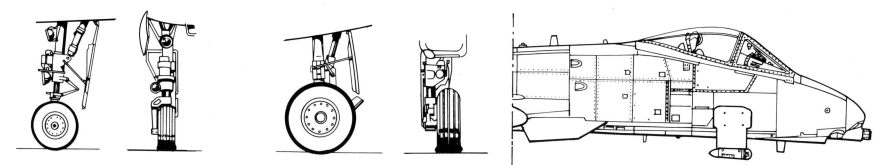

Nose Gear

Main Gear

Pave Penny

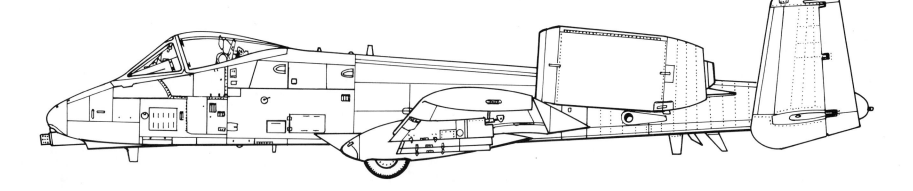

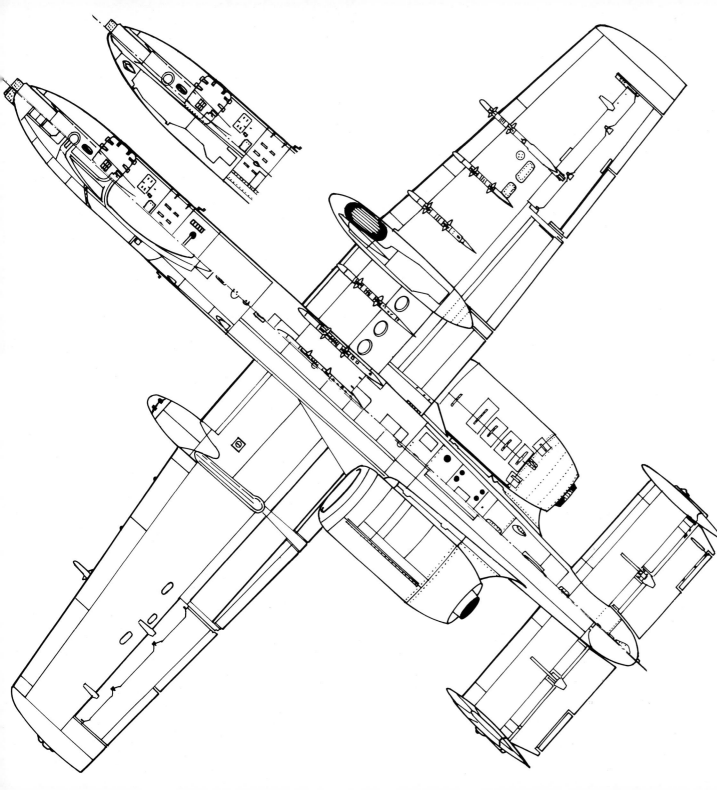

A-10 Warthog Specifications

Manufacturer	Fairchild Republic Co.
Primary Mission	Sustained close air support
Powerplant	Two General Electric TF34-GE-100 turbofan engines, each about 9,000 pounds (4,082 kg) of thrust
Length	53 feet, 4 inches (16.25m)
Height	14 feet, 8 inches (4.47m)
Wingspan	57 feet, 6 inches (17.53m)
Internal Fuel Capacity	10,700 pounds (4,853 kg)
Operating Weight	25,000 pounds (11,340 kg)
Maximum Gross Weight	50,000 pounds (22,680 kg)
Armament	One 30-mm. General Electric GAU-8 seven-barrel Gatling gun
Ammunition Capacity	1,174/1,350 rounds
Firing Rate	2100/4200 rounds per minute
Ordnance Capacity	Up to 16,000 pounds (7,257 kg) of mixed ordnance on ten underwing pylon stations with partial fuel. Can include both free-fall and precision-guided weapons, rockets, Maverick missiles, etc.
Take-off Distance with 4-500 lb. (227 kg) bombs, 750 rds. 30mm., 4,000 lbs. (1,814 kg) fuel	1,420 feet (433 m)
Distance at Max. Take-off Weight	4,000 feet (1,220 m)
Ferry Range without In-flight Refueling	2,173 nautical miles (4,026 km) into a 50 knot (93 km/hr) headwind
Combat speed with 6-500 lb. (227 kg) bombs, 750 rounds, 30 mm.	387 knots (717 km/hr)
Loiter Time with 250 NM (463 km) radius, 18-500 lb. (227 kg) bombs, 750 rounds 30 mm.	1.75 hours
Crew	Pilot only
Fire Control System	Head-up display, TV monitor and control, armament control system, and laser spot seeker set

17

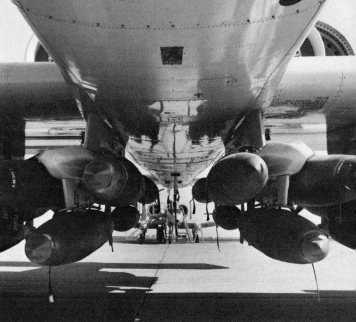

One of the primary anti-armor weapons employed by the A-10 is the electro-optically guided AGM-65B Maverick missile. Maverick has been in the tactical inventory since 1972 and has a performance record that averages close to 90% against tank-sized targets. (Shinichi Ohtaki)

Inert practice bombs loaded on the fuselage pylons of the prototype during initial flight testing to demonstrate load-carrying capability. (Fairchild Republic)

The *Pave Penny* pod, mounted on the right side of the fuselage is a laser seeker, used in conjunction with laser-guided munitions carried by the A-10, while an independent source illuminates the target with a designator. (Shinichi Ohtaki)

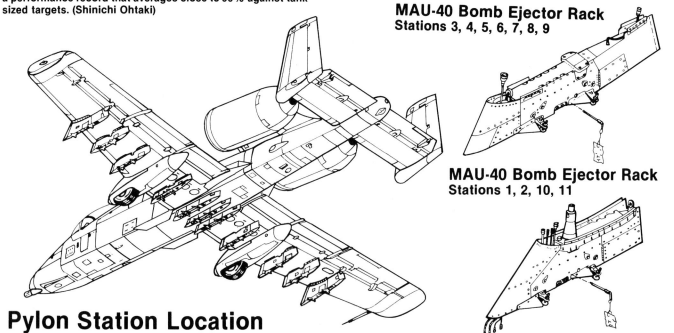

Pylon Station Location

MAU-40 Bomb Ejector Rack
Stations 3, 4, 5, 6, 7, 8, 9

MAU-40 Bomb Ejector Rack
Stations 1, 2, 10, 11

Weapons Capability

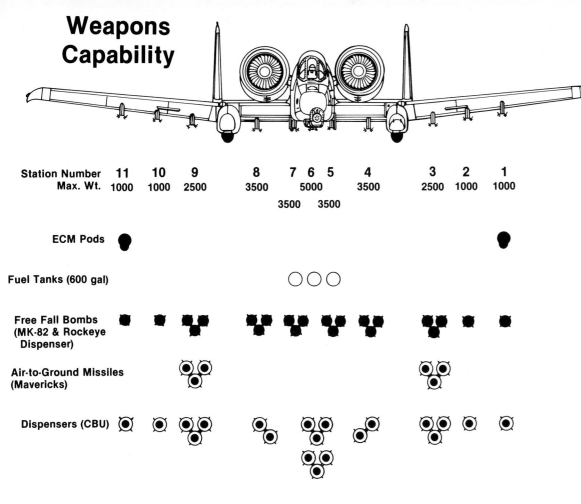

Station Number	11	10	9	8	7	6	5	4	3	2	1
Max. Wt.	1000	1000	2500	3500	5000			3500	2500	1000	1000
					3500		3500				

ECM Pods

Fuel Tanks (600 gal)

Free Fall Bombs (MK-82 & Rockeye Dispenser)

Air-to-Ground Missiles (Mavericks)

Dispensers (CBU)

Maximum Threat Anti-Armor Configuration

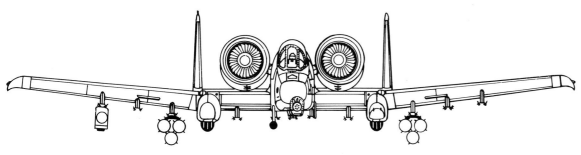

The A-10A was introduced to its more famous namesake at the official "naming" ceremony. (Fairchild Republic)

Tested on the A-10...the M-61 20MM Vulcan Gun Pod. (R.J. Mills, Jr.)

19

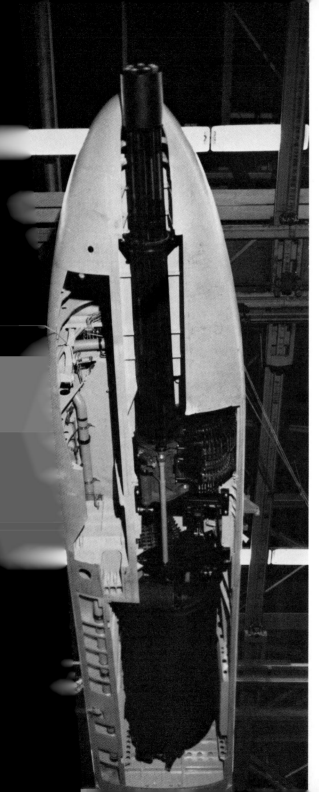

One of the most advanced features of the A-10 is its primary armament, the 30мм GAU-8A *Avenger* cannon. Everything about the Avenger is superlatives, from its size and weight, to its unbelievable destructive power. It uses an armor-piercing projectile of depleted uranium, which gives it an extremely high sectional density. High sectional density means a flatter trajectory, less effect by environmental elements, and greater retained kinetic energy. The Avenger is powered by a pair of hydraulic motors which, when used singly provide a firing rate of 2100 rounds per minute, and in tandem a rate of 4200 rounds per minute. At the max firing rate, the 1350 rounds of ammunition will last for 10 two second bursts. 81st TFW A-10s encountered a firing range problem, caused by the power of the 30мм rounds. Targets on the ranges are normally supported by telephone pole-sized posts. The GAU-8A's firing rate makes it impossible to avoid hitting these supports, which had been more than capable of withstanding 20мм hits in the past. However, one 30мм round is enough to shatter or uproot these telephone poles! Each group of seven barrels is estimated to have an average life of 21,000 rounds, while the weapon itself has demonstrated an average of 18,500 rounds between failures. (USAF and Fairchild Republic)

GAU-8A removed for maintenance at Myrtle Beach. Total weight of the gun and its drive mechanism is 740 lbs., while the ammunition and mount brings all-up weight of the system to over 4,000 lbs. Ease of maintenance of the A-10 systems is extraordinary. Inside of access panels is gloss grey. (Above left Norman E. Taylor) (Fairchild Republic)

(Above and Below) Having the refueling receptacle right in front of you simplifies hookup and station keeping during air-to-air refueling, whether it is on the KC-135 or KC-97L. (Fairchild Republic)

A pair of A-10As from the 354th TFW over the South Carolina countryside. (Fairchild Republic)

Initial color scheme for production A-10s was a two-tone grey of 50% mask 10A (light) and 30% mask 10A (dark), with all insignia and false canopy on fuselage bottom in gunship grey. Exceptions were made in individual units, such as this 354th TFW A-10, which has standard color TAC badge, and white tail band with dark green stars. (Norman E. Taylor)

A-10A of the 355th TFS, 354th TFW. Blade antennae under rear fuselage are UHF AM & FM radio which flank the fuel dump mast. Also visible are the radar homing and warning (RHAW) receivers mounted in the nose and tail. (Charles B. Mayer)

355th Tactical Fighter Wing

353 Fighter Squadron

333 TFTS

(Above Right and Right) Integral ECM equipment is the ALR-46 radar alarm system, which is augmented by carrying pods such as the ALQ-119 or ALQ-131 on external stations. Chaff dispensers are located underneath each wing tip. (Fairchild Republic)

23

A-10 during testing at Edwards AFB shows that it is not always ugly. (USAF via Mason)

A-10A of the 354th TFW at Myrtle Beach. Scoop under gun is for gun compartment venting, and outlets are immediately in front of ladder compartment, with large hole indicating location of extractor fan.

A-10A of the 354th rotating for practice mission. It carries practice bombs on MERs, ALQ-119 ECM pod, Maverick Missile launchers, with one AGM-65B Maverick. Underwing stations are all capable of handling TER's except for two outer stations, which will only accept MER's, or as in this case, Maverick launchers or ECM pods. (Shinichi Ohtaki)

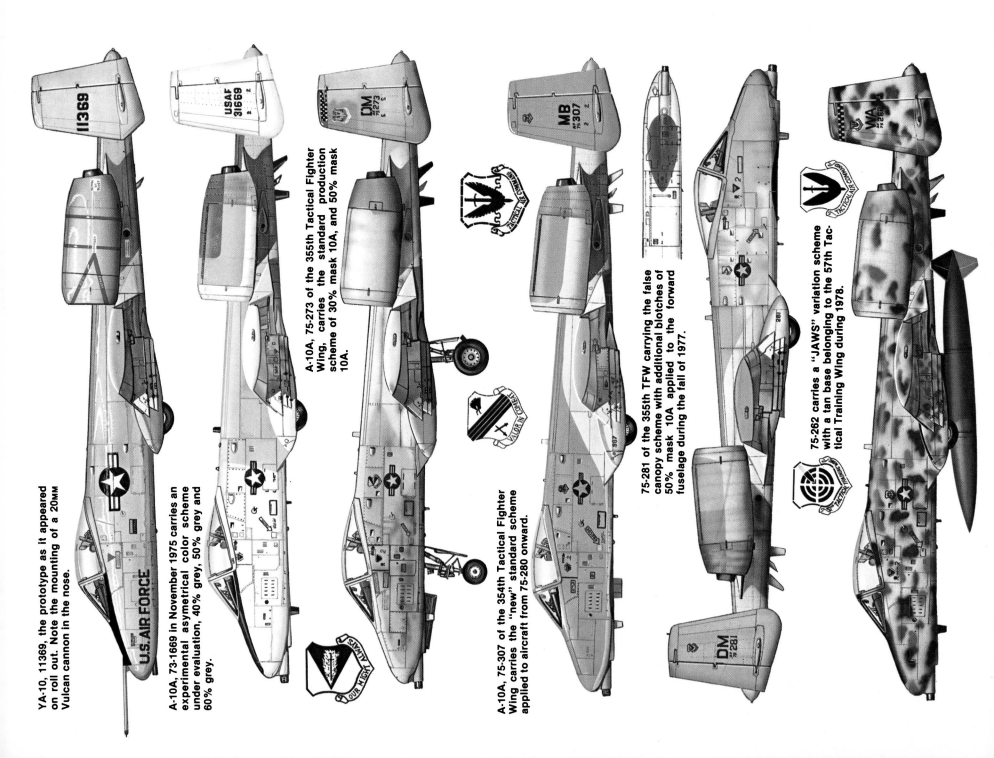

YA-10, 11369, the prototype as it appeared on roll out. Note the mounting of a 20mm Vulcan cannon in the nose.

A-10A, 73-1669 in November 1975 carries an experimental asymetrical color scheme under evaluation, 40% grey, 50% grey and 60% grey.

A-10A, 75-273 of the 355th Tactical Fighter Wing, carries the standard production scheme of 30% mask 10A, and 50% mask 10A.

A-10A, 75-307 of the 354th Tactical Fighter Wing carries the "new" standard scheme applied to aircraft from 75-280 onward.

75-281 of the 355th TFW carrying the false canopy scheme with additional blotches of 50% mask 10A applied to the forward fuselage during the fall of 1977.

75-262 carries a "JAWS" variation scheme with a tan base belonging to the 57th Tactical Training Wing during 1978.

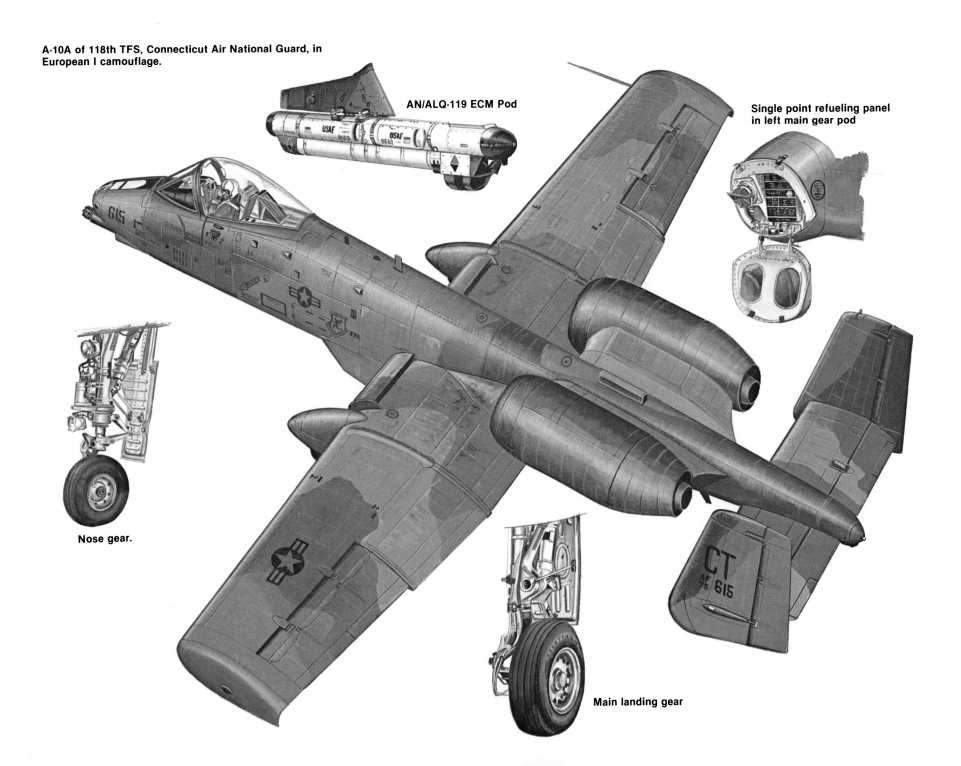

A-10A of 118th TFS, Connecticut Air National Guard, in European I camouflage.

AN/ALQ-119 ECM Pod

Single point refueling panel in left main gear pod

Nose gear.

Main landing gear

The fifth pre-production A-10A during weapons carrying tests at Edwards AFB, September 1975. It is loaded with 14 inert MK-82 low drag bombs.

**356th
Tactical Fighter
Squadron**

A-10A Serial Number 73-1669 being tested inside USAF Climatic Hangar at Eglin AFB, Florida. Note snow falling on aircraft while engines run. Virtually any climatic conditions encountered anywhere on earth can be duplicated in this facility, operated by Air Force Systems Command. (USAF via N.E. Taylor)

A-10A enroute to the United States, over England, returning from 1977 Paris Air Show. "44" was number assigned for the Paris Air Show. (USAF)

Hinged bullet-proof windscreen greatly aids in maintenance of the Kaiser heads-up display, which gives the pilot airspeed, altitude, pitch angle, and standard pipper information. (Shinichi Ohtaki)

(Above Right) A-10A landing at Myrtle Beach after a practice mission, during the 354th's transition from the A-7 to the A-10. (Shinichi Ohtaki)

**422d Fighter
Weapons Squadron**

(Middle Right) Leading edge slats on the A-10 are inboard of the wheel well pods, and are flanked by end plates and flow smoothing strakes on the fuselage. (Shinichi Ohtaki)

Single slotted, three position (up, maneuvering, landing) Fowler Flaps are shown in the full landing (down) position. (Shinichi Ohtaki)

A-10A of the 333rd TFTS, 355th TFW, Davis Monthan AFB, as it appeared in June 1977. (Charles B. Mayer)

A-10A of the 358th TFTS, 355th TFW, Davis Monthan, at the Offut AFB open house in August 1978. Pod on centerline is for carriage of baggage during RON, and is used on several different types of aircraft. (Charles B. Mayer)

75-264 of the 333rd TFTS carried a slightly different pattern of the mask 10A scheme while on a 1976 European Tour, Ramstein AB, Germany, September 1976. (Joos via J. Geer)

A-10A with a multiplicity of safety pin ribbons hanging from empty triple ejector racks. Note vent under windscreen, which directs air under pressure to clear rain. (Fairchild Republic)

Firing the GAU-8 gun. Also carried on this mission are the HOBOS 2,000 lb. TV guided bomb and the Paveway 3,000 lb. Laser Guided Bomb. (USAF)

N/AW A-10A

Though barely operational, the A-10 had become the United States' main anti-armor weapon. Since the Soviet Bloc devotes 35 to 40% of its time to night training, it is reasonable to assume that any attack they launched might come in the dark. In order to attack such a force, the VFR-oriented A-10 would have to operate under flares, and would be effectively grounded in low ceilings and visibilities. Half the effectiveness of the number one tank killer could be negated by weather and/or darkness. In order to solve that problem, Fairchild went to work on a two-seat version of the Warthog, which they designated the Night/Adverse Weather A-10. With two million dollars of company funds, and 7.5 million dollars of DOD independent research and development funds, they modified the first of the preproduction A-10As (73-1664) into a two-seater. In addition to the second seat for the Weapons System Officer, Forward Looking Infrared Radar, Low Light Level Television, Lasar Rangefinder, Radar Altimeter, and the Westinghouse WX-50 multimode radar was added to the basic aircraft. The WX-50 is capable of terrain-following, ground mapping, and threat detection. The two-seater made its first flight on 4 May 1979, at a gross weight of 2,091 lbs. more than the A-10A. The test program lasted for five months, and included 120 hours of flying. Fairchild also used the two-seater to squire various and sundry dignitaries around the Edwards complex, suitably impressing them with its low level dexterity. As of this writing, no firm decision has been made on the future of the two-seater.

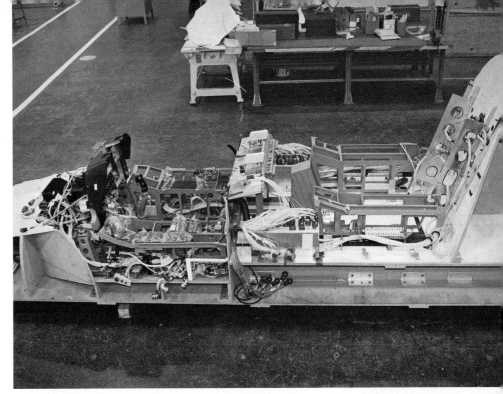

Work-up on the cockpit of the company-funded two seat Night/Adverse weather A-10. (Fairchild Republic)

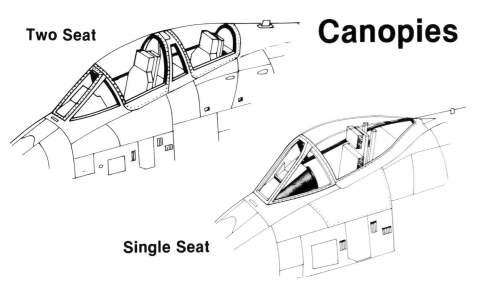

Canopies

Two Seat

Single Seat

The complete modification of the one A-10A into the two seat version took 13 months. Side hinged canopies are simpler, hence cheaper and lighter, and they will be installed on single seat versions in the future. (Fairchild Republic)

Two seater over the California desert during evalutation at Edwards. (Fairchild Republic)

Forward Looking Infrared unit was carried in a pod on the center line during evaluations. If a production two seater is built, this unit will be housed in the right wheel well pod, which will be extended to accommodate it. (Fairchild Republic)

Rear instrument panel, with Forward Looking Infrared display on top of panel, radar, and video map displays immediately below. (Fairchild Republic)

The Night/Adverse Weather A-10 at Edwards during the test program. It is finished in overall Gunship Grey FS36118. (Fairchild Republic)

Rudder Development

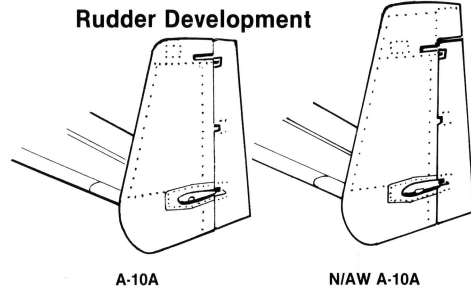

A-10A   **N/AW A-10A**

De-stabilizing effect of the deeper front fuselage was negated by adding 20 inches to the top of each vertical fin. The rear seat is 10 inches higher than the front, allowing the rear seater some chance at looking over the pilot's shoulder. Though it is assumed that a production two seater would carry a WSO in the rear, the prototype is fitted with full dual controls, including emergency gear extension provision. Duties of the WSO would include navigation via the INS and radar ground mapping, monitoring of RHAW gear, operation of the FLIR, operation of ECM gear, and designation of targets.

The N/AW A/10A prototype unbuttoned to demonstrate ease of maintenance.

The side-opening canopy will be installed on the single seat version in later production runs.

Specifications

	N/AW A-10	A-10A
Take-off gross weight	44,162 lb	43,071 lb
Combat radius	246 n.m.	252 n.m.
Maximum speed	365kt	368kt
Sustained load factor*	3 • 2g	3 • 4g
Instantaneous load factor*	6 • 1g	6 • 5g
Take-off ground roll	2,820ft	2,530ft
Landing ground roll	1,220ft	1,140ft

*Load factors at 300kt.

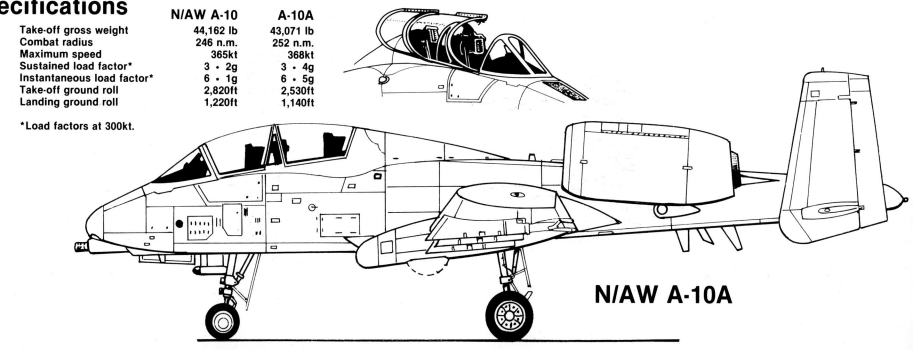

N/AW A-10A

**355th TAC
Fighter Squadron**

Be it known to all men present, that

_____

"did it in the bathtub" for the first time on _____ A.D.
and proved, once again, that A-10 pilots have a bigger gun.
attest _____

358th TFTS

This factory fresh A-10 shows off its offset nose gear clearly. Wing leading edges, flap shrouds, control surfaces and tail leading edges are nomex core honeycomb, with alloy skins for fire resistance and strength. (Fairchild Republic)

JOINT ATTACK WEAPONS SYSTEM

As the first aircraft designed from the ground up as a pure close air support machine, the A-10 has helped to develop and refine a whole new set of tactics. These tactics have evolved through the *Joint Attack Weapons Systems* tests (JAWS) held at Fort Hunter Liggett, California. Several experimental camouflage systems were devised and applied during these tests, though none of them were adopted. The basic tactical premise during JAWS was complete integration of the A-10 and Army Aviation units. When the A-10's and the Cobra Helicopter gunships worked together, kill ratios on tanks went up three and four times. (Monterey Peninsula Herald via Fairchild Republic)

Every known Warsaw Pact Anti-aircraft threat was simulated during JAWS, including use of an Aggressor Squadron F-5 from Nellis AFB, acting as a MiG-21. Most of the action took place below 1,000 feet, with the A-10s using terrain masking, while Cobras hid behind trees waiting until AAA was lured into firing at the A-10 before popping up for its shots. Scout helicopters were used to pre-select targets. A-10s flew in flights of two, but did not fly formation, since it was quickly determined that the wingman was a sitting duck if forced to fly on the leader during the fight. Instead, they coordinated their attacks with the helicopters, attempting to ensure constant pressure on the enemy, from all compass points. The necessity for pilots in excellent physical condition was proven in these tests also. At low level and relatively high air speeds, maneuverability means pulling a lot of Gs. A-10 pilots were instrumented for heart, respiration, and blood pressure during the tests. Aircraft accelerometers showed up to 7 positive and 2 negative Gs. Mission stresses are likely to exceed those endured by the Astronauts...and several times a day during a shooting war! The Joint Attack Team concept that emerged from JAWS should enable outnumbered U.S. forces to stall the enemy attack. In addition to the helicopter gunships, the team will also rely heavily on the Army's artillery and mortar units to maintain constant pressure on the attackers. (Photos by David Lindsay, Fort Ord Panorama via Fairchild Republic)

Though no live ammunition was used during the initial JAWs exercises, every aircraft and vehicle was linked to Fort Hunter Liggett's Range Measuring System (RMS), a sophisticated computer that measured hits or misses based on known weapons capabilites and the parameters under which the weapons were fired. The RMS was used to simulate enemy weapons capabilities, as well as the weapons carried by the A-10s and Cobras. In addition to the dust churned up by maneuvering vehicles, blank cannon shells were fired, creating a more realistic battlefield atmosphere. Missions were flown in the morning most of the time, with debriefings and mission critiques, using RMS and gun camera data, consuming the balance of each day. (David Lindsay, Fort Ord Panorama via Fairchild Republic)

A-10A of the 66th Fighter Weapons Squadron, 57th Tactical Training Wing, Nellis AFB. Mask 10A grey scheme, somewhat mottled by weathering, with yellow/black checkerboard on tail, TAC and 57th Patch are in standard colors.

(Above & Below) The first Warthogs assigned to Europe arrived in January, 1979 in the then standard two tone grey camouflage. They belonged to the 92nd TFS, 81st TFW, based at RAF Bentwaters-Woodbridge, UK. They were immediately flown to Forward Operating Locations (FOL's) in Germany to begin training over the terrain they would have to defend in war. Four FOL's in Germany were selected, including Sembach, Noervenich, Leipheim, and Ahlhorn. Semback was the first FOL activated. As a base for OV-10s, work with FAC's familiar with the geography was greatly enhanced. (Peter Bennett and Robert J. Archer)

The operational camouflage scheme eventually adopted for the A-10 was initially dubbed "Lizard" and consisted of FS36081 dark gray, FS34102 light green, and FS34092 dark green. It was later officially named "European I" and has been applied to several other aircraft as well, including the OV-10A, O-2, UH-1, CH-3, and H-53. All A-10s roll out of the factory in Europe I, regardless of where they are destined to spend their operational lives. (Fairchild Republic)

Anti-Armor Close Air Support Mission

Full Internal Fuel 10,700 lbs.
Standard Day

Combat: 30 Mins
Max. Cont. Power, S.L.

Cruise Out & Back
at 5000 ft

40 NM

I.P.

S.L. Penetration
and Exit

230 NM

Landing
Reserve
20 Mins.
S.L.

Ordnance Loading

6 Mavericks
1 ALQ-119 ECM Pod
Full Complement of
30mm Ammunition
480 Flare/Chaff Units

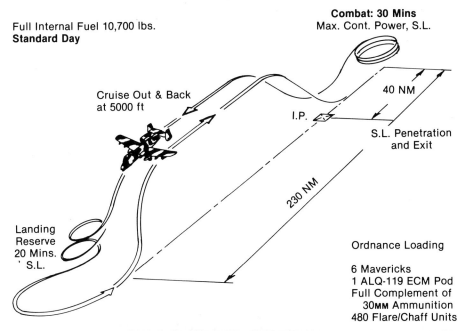

The business end of the 30mm GAU-8 by General Electric. (Ted Carson)

A-10A of the 131st TFS, Massachusetts Air National Guard. (Brian Rogers via Jerry Geer)

A-10A with the markings of the 81st TFW, ready for the long ferry flight from Davis Monthan, fitted with the 600 gallon long range auxiliary fuel tanks. (Brian Rogers via Jerry Geer)

A-10A of the 333rd TFTS, 355th TFW, Davis Monthan, as it appeared in December 1979. Red and white checkerboard on tail, practice bombs on centerline MERs. (Brian Rogers via Jerry Geer)

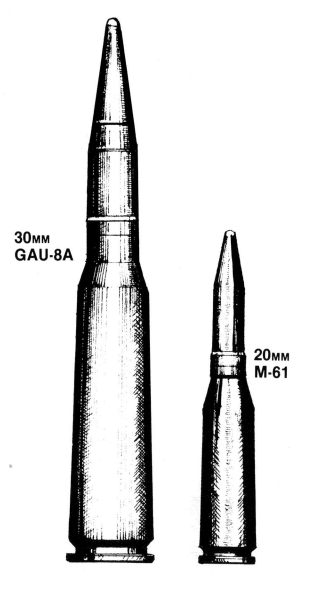

30ᴍᴍ
GAU-8A

20ᴍᴍ
M-61

Uploading 30ᴍᴍ ammunition for the GAU-8A Avenger cannon at Myrtle Beach AFB, April 1980. The only piece of ground support equipment that is exclusively A-10 is the Coloney Company's Ammunition Loading System, (ALS) which allows a full load of 30ᴍᴍ ammunition to be loaded within 13 minutes. Combined with the reliability of the gun system, (one stoppage in three months of daily live-fire exercises by the 81st TFW from RAF Bentwaters) this will give the A-10 mission turn-around times that were unheard of with previous close support aircraft. (Norman E. Taylor)

A-10s of the 354th TFW, Myrtle Beach AFB, S.C. Several A-10s remained in grey camouflage when the photo at top was taken in April 1980. When it was decided to change to "Europe I" camouflage, the prime overhaul facility for the Air Force, at McClelland AFB, California came up with a figure of $23,000 per airplane. The 354th was able to accomplish the task, using local civilian labor, for $3,300 per airplane, thus saving the tax payers over a million dollars, and getting the job done a year sooner than if they had to ferry the airplanes to McClelland! The paint used in the Europe I scheme is a specially designed radar-absorbing polyurethane, made famous as a part of the "stealth" technology. (Norm Taylor, Brian Rogers via Jerry Geer, and Fairchild Republic)

A-10A of the 354th TFW at Myrtle Beach AFB, S.C., November 1980. Note that unit pride has restored full colors to TAC and 354th badges, and that tail bands are white with green stars. Low visibility camouflage schemes can be carried too far! It is also fitted with the Pave Penny laser signal seeking pod on right side of nose. (Norman E. Taylor)

The 23rd TFW has continued their tradition of arming their aircraft with teeth, with a notable prerequisite. Each aircraft has to fly 35 missions before earning its fangs. 70-0139 is the Wing CO's airplane, as indicated by the squadron colors on each vertical fin and rudder. (23rd TFW via N.E. Taylor)

66th Fighter Weapons School

(Far Left and Left) A-10s of the 354th TFW over South Carolina on training flights. Low level, high G maneuvers produce condensation vortices as the A-10 above pulls off the target. (USAF)

Operation of the split ailerons as speed brakes is evident in this shot of a 353rd TFS War-thog landing at Myrtle Beach AFB, November 1980. (Norm Taylor)

Ground crewmen install one of the new AN/ALQ-119(V) ECM pods on the number one accessory rack of a Massachusetts ANG A-10A, prior to squadron participation in Red Flag exercise at Nellis AFB, November and December 1980. (Norm Taylor)

A-10A of the 131st TFS, MASS ANG: at Myrtle Beach AFB, November 1980. (Norm Taylor)

(Above) A Warthog of the 131st TFS taxis out at Myrtle Beach, enroute to Nellis in November 1980. It is fitted with the long range ferry tank on the centerline. The A-10 will equip some Air Force Reserve units as well as Air National Guard units, making these stand-by units more combat capable than ever before. First AFRES units to get the A-10 will be the 45th TFS, Grissom AFB, Indiana, (replacing A-37s) and the 47th TFS at Barksdale AFB, La. (also replacing A-37s). (Norman E. Taylor)

(Below) The two-seater, as seen at Davis Monthan AFB in March, 1980 during a refueling stop enroute to Eglin AFB Florida for additional AFSC testing. Note that the instrumented nose probe has been removed, and that the Pave Penny pod has a nose cap in place to protect it during the long ferry flight. (Brian Rogers via Norman E. Taylor)

Aircraft Armor Weapons Warships

squadron/signal
publications

in action